Encouraging Reading

Also available from Continuum

Beginning Reading, Yola Center

Pocket PAL: Boys and Writing, Stephen Bowkett

Foundations of Literacy, Sue Palmer and Ros Bayley

101 Essential Lists for Secondary Teachers, Susan Elkin

Help Your Child with Literacy, Caroline Coxon

Flying Start with Literacy, Ros Bayley and Lynn Broadbent

Teaching Assistant's Guide to Literacy, Susan Elkin

Encouraging Reading

Susan Elkin

Ideas in Action

network
continuum

Published by Network Continuum Education

The Tower Building
11 York Road
London
SE1 7NX

80 Maiden Lane, Suite 704
New York, NY 10038

www.networkcontinuum.co.uk
www.continuumbooks.com

An imprint of The Continuum International Publishing Group Ltd.

British Library Cataloguing-in-Publication Data
A catalogue record for this book is available from the British Library.

ISBN: 9781855393509 (paperback)

Library of Congress Cataloging-in-Publication Data
A catalogue record for this book is available from the Library of Congress.

Typeset by
Bookens Ltd, Royston, Herts
Printed and bound in Great Britain by
Antony Rowe Ltd, Chippenham, Wiltshire

For my granddaughters, Charlotte and Jasmine Elkin

Contents

Introduction

This is not a book about learning to read. It's a book about transforming new readers into real readers and keeping up the momentum. It's also about helping children of all ages to enjoy books of all sorts.

Nearly all children – without severe disability – eventually learn to turn the squiggles on the page, paper or noticeboard into words. They may not be very quick or fluent, but when they see *Danger!* or *Menu*, they know what it means. Very few people in the modern developed world reach adulthood in a state of total illiteracy.

By age seven, most children can stumble through a passage from a book while an adult listens – simple decoding. I would argue that actually this is not reading and that real reading is what you learn to do once you have cracked the code.

It's like swimming. Getting your 10-metre certificate is not the end of your swimming career. It's the beginning. Now that you can stay afloat and use a stroke or two to propel yourself along, you can strike out, build up your swimming stamina and enjoy the water. It's just the same with reading. We have to help children to grow into strong, confident deep-end readers.

Sadly, this is a stage and a concept which is often neglected. It's easy to think that once Chloë or Zach can read, the job is done. You can tick the reading box and hurry on to the next thing. But if you passed your driving test, walked out of the test centre and didn't get behind the wheel again for five or ten years, you would probably find that the driving skill had gone because you hadn't consolidated and developed it.

There is also work to be done to catch the boy or girl who loses interest in reading when puberty kicks in. Boys in particular need careful managing because they are less likely to take to fiction than their sisters, so teachers have to find other ways of keeping them hooked.

Fast fluent readers don't subvocalize. Subvocalizers read every word aloud to themselves in their heads, but without speaking. A strong 'deep-end' reader can read quickly for meaning without having to 'translate' each individual word into a sound. The brain learns to convert signs seen by the eye into meaning without consciously passing through the medium of spoken or heard words.

We need to move the subvocalizers on. That's why learners need blocks of time every day when they read independently and silently. As with any other skill, the more you do it the faster you get. It's partly a matter of acquiring the confidence to stop using subvocalizing as a prop.

Need evidence that books still matter in this digital age? In 2003 a study in 37 countries by the Programme for International Student Assessment (PISA) found that the most important factor for academic success was the amount of time pupils spent reading – books, magazines, newspapers and websites. But it's time spent reading books which makes the biggest difference, according to this and several other studies.

This book suggests ways of getting school children to read more. Reading, once you can do it well, is an endless source of pleasure. It is also the key to every other sort of learning.

1 Fiction

Early years

When they are under seven, many children will still be learning to decode the letters and words on a page, and some will already be fluent readers. The important thing at this stage is to lay the foundations for the enjoyment of reading and the confident ongoing love of books.

This means that, as well as learning phonics so that they can decode accurately, pupils must hear lots of stories – and other information – read aloud from books.

Many classrooms have book corners. There is a regular story slot each day. Children are encouraged to pick up and look at books. Adults (teachers, classroom assistants, nursery nurses and so on) spend a lot of time looking at books with the children. There should be books in the classroom which children can borrow and take home. They should be encouraged to read to each other and/or to toys. As they get older, more and more of the children will be able to read independently – so set time aside for it.

Books are great; books are fun; books are vital to our learning. If you can get this message across to under-sevens, there's every chance it will stick.

Advice

Children love stories. So, for many children, fiction is the way in to reading. The more we capitalize on this love of narrative, the more likely children are to become keen readers.

There are many hundreds of books which very young children love sharing. You will have your own favourites and so will the children. Here are just a few recommendations. Like many books at this level, these all, in their different ways, have wonderful illustrations:

- *Jinnie Ghost* by Jane Ray and Berlie Doherty (Frances Lincoln)
- *Rosie's Walk* by Pat Hutchins (Red Fox)
- *Lost and Found* by Oliver Jeffers (HarperCollins)
- *Miffy* series by Dick Bruna (Egmont)
- *Russell the Sheep* by Rob Scotton (HarperCollins)
- *10 Little Rubber Ducks* by Eric Carle (HarperCollins)
- *The Big Sneeze* by Ruth Brown (Andersen Press).

When you read aloud, point to the words as you go along. It shows the children what you are reading from and reminds them that written words carry meaning. The more advanced readers will recognize some of the words you are pointing to.

Slightly older children might like:

- *James and the Giant Peach* by Roald Dahl (Puffin)
- *Just So Stories* by Rudyard Kipling (various publishers)
- *Mixed Up Fairy Tales* by Hilary Robinson and Nick Sharratt (Hodder)
- *The Gruffalo* by Julia Donaldson and Axel Scheffler (Macmillan)
- *Mog the Forgetful Cat* by Judith Kerr (HarperCollins).

Application

Ages 7–11

Most children can decode by this age. What they need now is lots of time to read, and plenty of upbeat encouragement from the adults in the classroom. It will help if you have read the titles you want the children to read. Then you and they can chat about the books.

If you and a pupil have both read, for example, *The Amazing Story of Adolphus Tips* by Michael Morpurgo (HarperCollins), you could tell each other whether you think the title really fits the story, or what you thought about the present-day ending. It is very encouraging for children to discover that an adult has read some of 'their' books.

From thousands of possibilities, I've picked just a handful of premier-league fiction titles and authors to suggest here. Start your own journey into children's fiction with some of these if you haven't already read them.

I've divided the recommendations into approximate age bands on this and the next few pages, but be aware that these age ranges are very fluid. A nine year old will sometimes happily read a book more usually read by 13 year olds, and vice versa. Remember that reading levels, ability and interest don't have much to do with chronological age and no two children are the same.

Some children respond well to sitting in a reading group in which all the children are reading the same title independently. Then, when they have all finished, they can discuss it, prepare a talk for the rest of the class about it, design a wall poster advertising it, act out part of the story – and many other group activities.

A few suggested titles to recommend to children are listed below. Some of these are tried and tested old favourites which have become classics. Others are more recent.

- *Skellig* by David Almond (Hodder)
- *The Silver Sword* by Ian Serraillier (Red Fox)
- *Goodnight Mister Tom* by Michelle Magorian (Puffin)
- *Simone's Letters* by Helena Pielichaty (OUP)
- *Tom's Midnight Garden* by Philippa Pearce (Puffin)
- *I, Coriander* by Sally Gardner (Puffin/Orion)
- *The Amazing Story of Adolphus Tips* by Michael Morpurgo (HarperCollins)
- *The Cat Mummy* by Jacqueline Wilson (Corgi)
- *A Bear Called Paddington* by Michael Bond (Collins)

Other authors who write very well for this age group include:

- Francesca Simon
- Sharon Creech
- Beverly Cleary
- Ursula Le Guin
- Anne Fine
- Lynne Reid Banks
- Sally Prue
- Geraldine McCaughrean.

Ages 11–14

This age group is particularly tricky. A boy or girl of 11 might still read quite 'babyish' books. Three years – and an adolescence – later at age 14, he or she may be reading books published for adults. Children all develop at different rates and this is particularly noticeable at these ages. So, it is impossible to generalize across these three years.

Therefore, read as many books written for this age group as you can. You will soon develop a feeling for what is likely to appeal to which child and therefore what to recommend.

Be aware that fantasy – from Terry Pratchett to J.K. Rowling – is very popular with many young people. That is why over half of all the fiction now published for teenagers is fantasy-based. Yet many adults – especially teachers and librarians – don't warm to it. Don't let this impede your encouragement of the students. Say something like, 'Well, I've read Marianne Curley's *Old Magic* and it didn't do a lot for me. But I know that many people have enjoyed it. Do you think you will like it? / What did you like about it?'

Be honest and open-minded. Apart from anything else, you are teaching the students that much of what is 'good' or 'bad' about a book is down to personal taste and no two people are the same. However, never condemn something a student has read and enjoyed ('That book's rubbish') just because you didn't enjoy it. It's insulting and hurtful and not likely to encourage reading.

Develop a culture in which students respect each other's reading too.

These are some titles that might appeal to you and to your 11–14-year-old students:

- *Tamar* by Mal Peet (Walker Books)
- *Wolf* by Gillian Cross (OUP/Puffin)
- *The Foreshadowing* by Marcus Sedgwick (Orion)
- *His Dark Materials* three-book series by Philip Pullman (Scholastic)
- *The Hobbit* by J.R.R. Tolkien (various publishers)
- *Private Peaceful* by Michael Morpurgo (HarperCollins)
- *Noughts and Crosses* by Malorie Blackman (Corgi)
- *Al Capone Does My Shirts* by Gennifer Choldenko (Bloomsbury).

Look too for suitable books by:

- Robert Cormier
- Kevin Crossley Holland
- Adèle Geras
- Geraldine McCaughrean
- Bernard Ashley
- Robert Westall
- Cynthia Voight
- Mildred D. Taylor
- Jill Paton Walsh
- James Riordan.

Ages 15+

It is 'cool' adult behaviour to read. What, after all, do the majority of passengers do on trains and planes? If they are awake, many of them will be reading – usually novels.

Many students at this level will be studying fiction works for exams. Build on this by enthusing about other related books. For example:

- John Steinbeck's *Of Mice and Men* could lead to *The Pearl*, *The Red Pony* and *East of Eden*.

- *Roll of Thunder* and *Hear My Cry* could mean interest in the sequels and prequels in Mildred E. Taylor's series.

- *Cat's Eye* might inspire students to move on to other fiction by Margaret Atwood and then other Canadian writers such as Carol Shields.

See every curriculum book as a starting point, not as an end. And, even if you're not the English teacher, take a hands-on (or eyes-down) interest in students' curriculum and related reading. It will give you common ground with those you work with.

Reluctant older readers can sometimes be motivated by helping younger students with reading difficulties. The older student can listen to the younger one read; read aloud to him or her; or help with a book-related activity. In schools which have set up programmes to encourage this, the reading levels of both reading partners have improved. The younger one enjoys the individual attention, and the status of being a reader-helper can work wonders for the self-esteem and confidence of the older student.

Advice

Students aged 15 upwards will enjoy some of the books by these fiction writers who specialize in the upper end of the 'children's' market:

- Aidan Chambers
- Linda Newbery
- Mal Peet
- Michelle Magorian.

They will also enjoy old favourites and classics originally written for adults, such as:

- *Gone With the Wind* by Margaret Mitchell
- *Rebecca* by Daphne Du Maurier
- *Jane Eyre* by Charlotte Brontë
- *Silas Marner* by George Eliot.

Contemporary writers whose books appeal to mid-teens include:

- Joanna Trollope
- Frederick Forsyth
- Ruth Rendell
- Stephen King
- John Grisham.

Many of this age group, particularly boys, still enjoy anything by Arthur Conan Doyle.

Application

Setting an example

Children imitate adults. That is how they learn.

If children see adults absorbed in and enjoying books, they get the message that reading is a grown-up thing to do. If, on the other hand, adults in positions of influence – such as teachers – say they are too busy to read because they have other more important things to do, children are likely to stop reading at the earliest opportunity because not reading 'feels' like grown-up behaviour.

This is one very significant reason why so many under-12s read quite enthusiastically, but give up as soon as they hit puberty.

It is therefore essential for young people to see lots of adult 'role models' reading books. Sadly, they may not have this at home (although many will), so school has to compensate.

Advice

- Always have a book with you that you are in the process of reading – sticking out of your bag or on the corner of your desk. Make it clear that you take your book wherever you go in case you get an odd moment.
- Let the children see you reading for pleasure.
- If the class or group is reading silently (see page 20), then you should read too. If you undertake any other activity, you are suggesting that it is more important than reading. It isn't (except in the direst of emergencies such as to tend a sick child).
- Take opportunities to talk informally to the children about books and reading.
- Become a book eccentric (book buff?, book nut?). Poke a little fun at yourself. Present yourself as someone who:
  - never leaves home bookless
  - has sold your television set
  - sometimes forgets to wash up because you are so deep in your book
  - often can't remember whether you've read the book or seen the film...

The children will laugh at you, but also with you. They will also admire your respect and enthusiasm for the printed word, and some will copy it.

- Tell the children about books you enjoyed when you were their age and/or about books your own children have liked.
- Encourage children to tell you about books they have read and you haven't, and listen to what they say. Make a point of reading some of the books suggested and then feeding back your thoughts. It is very gratifying for a child if a teacher heeds a recommendation and spends time exploring it. It gives reading real status.

Author visits

Many authors of children's books take time to visit schools to talk to pupils about the books they have written and to encourage children to read. Often, they will spend a whole day in a school working with different groups.

Young people get very excited about meeting authors – the faces behind the names on the covers of books – and such meetings are a powerful way of encouraging reading.

Children will want to read some of the books before they meet a writer. Or, if they have already read some, they will be motivated and curious to read other books after meeting the author. Most authors bring copies of their books with them so that children – advised in advance to bring some money – can buy a copy and get it signed. (Or you could invite parents to the events and let them do the buying.) Authors will also usually sign copies of their books that the children or school already own.

As self-employed people, authors visiting schools do, of course, have to charge for their time, so, if such an event isn't included in your school budget you will need to find a way of paying for it. The school's Parent Teacher Association (PTA) might help, for instance, or there might be a local business that would sponsor the meeting.

When you do have it all organized, don't forget to invite the local newspaper in to take some pictures. Author visits are quite high profile and it will be a feather in your cap with the headteacher if you can get some good, positive publicity for the school and its pupils.

Advice

There are several ways of contacting writers to invite them to visit your school:

- Approach the publisher which produces their books (publisher contact details are printed at the front of all books).
- The National Association of Writers in Education has a directory on its website (nawe.co.uk) of authors who make school visits.
- The Society of Authors may also be able to help (societyofauthors.co.uk).
- Another useful website is ContactAnAuthor.co.uk.
- In the USA, http://usawrites4kids.drury.edu is a good source of information and advice.

You can sometimes get help through Arts Councils who have some funds to support this sort of work:

- England: artscouncil.org.uk
- Northern Ireland: artscouncil-ni.org
- Scotland: scottisharts.org.uk
- Wales: artswales.org.uk.

The National Literacy Trust has helpful advice about authors in schools on its website, literacytrust.org.uk.

A school's Parent Teacher Association (PTA) or a local business will sometimes sponsor an author visit.

If you invite another school to share the visit, you can also share the cost.

Application

Libraries and bookshops

Most schools have a library, be it large or small. The smallest primary school library is teacher-managed. Some big secondary schools have a qualified librarian on the staff. At Reception and Key Stage 1 – and sometimes at Key Stage 2 – there will also be book corners or class libraries.

In secondary schools, English department book boxes are a good idea too. These can be a resource purchased by the English department, or be loaned to the department and changed regularly by the school library. Students borrow from them for independent reading. At their best, they offer material at a wide range of reading levels in fiction and non-fiction.

The purpose of all this is, of course, to make as many books available as possible to the pupils in order to encourage wider, quicker, more frequent and more committed reading.

Schools often also run book shops or clubs through which books, often at discounted prices or with profits to the school fund, are sold to pupils as another way of raising the profile of reading.

Some independent bookshops (sadly these are an endangered species these days) will provide stock on a sale or return basis. The National Literacy Trust has a useful list of specialist children's bookshops on its website (literacytrust.org.uk/familyreading/parents/bookshops.html).

Alternatively, you can work through a book supplier such as Bags of Books (bags-of-books.co.uk) or Bookspread Ltd (bookspread.co.uk).

Advice

Learners of any age can benefit from a visit to the public library as part of routine curriculum work.

Many children come from families for whom library use and books are not part of life. So, they do not know what is inside the library and what it can offer.

Set up your visit by arrangement with the library staff. Then pupils will be able to meet the children's librarian and other staff, see the facilities and discover that there are many more books, and perhaps better facilities, there than at school.

Library staff are usually willing to organize an introductory session for school groups and to show them around the library. Many libraries run after-school and holiday events for children. Particularly at primary level, if you can get the children excited about the library, they might work on their parents to take them there afterwards.

Hooking your pupils up with the public library is yet another way of getting them to regard reading as part of life. It maximizes their exposure to books and introduces them to other adults who regard books as really important.

Because library books are shared books, they also encourage readers to discuss titles and recommend them to each other.

Application

Book reviews

Book reviews can promote or deepen children's interest in stories and novels.

Reading reviews

All newspapers and many magazines (including specialist ones such as *The School Librarian*, *Books for Keeps* and *Carousel*) carry reviews of books for children and young people. There are websites too offering good, impartial reviews, such as http://books.guardian.co.uk/childrenslibrary. The National Literacy Trust has a list of websites which review children's books (literacytrust.org.uk/campaign/Booklists.html). Remember that the publishing industry categorizes any book aimed at under-16s as a children's book.

You can often trigger an interest in a book by reading, or showing, children a review of it. Depending on the age of the learners, you might then pin the review on a noticeboard and/or put a link to it on the school's intranet – not forgetting to ensure that there are copies of the book available in the classroom or school library so that any interested reader can get it easily.

Writing reviews

Children also learn from writing their own reviews (or giving them as oral presentations) so that they are encouraged to reflect on their reading and recommend books to each other. It is best not to be judgemental about their choices though. Within reason, let children share the books they really enjoyed. The idea is to get them reading freely and eclectically. Later, once they have become compulsive readers, you can drip-feed awareness of 'better', or more challenging, books if you need to.

Give the children's reviews as much status as you can to show that you take their reading and their views very seriously. Publish reviews in the school magazine or on a class web page, or build them into an assembly, for example.

Writing a book review is a specific skill. As with any other form of writing, the best way to learn to do it well is to read lots of professional reviews.

Learners need to grasp the following guidelines for reviewing fiction. You can adapt them for different age groups and allow writers some flexibility, but the principles are always the same:

● Retell a bit of the story, perhaps from near the beginning, but don't give away too much – and never reveal the ending.

● Mention an incident or two which you found especially interesting, exciting, striking, mysterious, tantalizing...

● Comment on one or two memorable characters and how well you think the author has depicted them.

● Work into your writing a clear understanding of what kind of book it is – fantasy, family, animal, historical, and so on.

● Never copy from the book jacket blurb. Your review must be all your own ideas.

● Say something about the writing style. Does the book have a narrator? Is the language chatty and conversational or fairly formal?

● Comment on the illustrations if applicable.

● Summarize what you liked or disliked about the book and why you would recommend it or not. Be very precise: 'I loved Nicky Singer's *GemX* because it shows realistically what the effects of human genetic modification could be and I'd never thought about that properly before', not '*GemX* is good and I enjoyed it'.

● Remember that you should say a lot in a short review. Every word should tell the potential reader something about the book.

Six things to do with a novel

If you, and a group or class, are reading a novel together – that is, all reading the same title at once – how are you going to share the reading, learning and shared experience?

The problem with shared reading of a full-length novel is that it tends to take a long time – several weeks if you read a chapter a day for example.

So, there are two challenges. First, you have to decide how to organize the reading. Will you read it aloud to the class while they follow, or get class members to take it in turns to read aloud? Or will they read some chapters in companionable silence and then read a section aloud when everyone has reached it? Will you ask them to read the occasional chapter for homework? Or do you favour a combination of all these – or some other method?

The solution, of course, depends on the size, age and reading ability of the group. And there are always some pupils who are frustrated (fast readers) or left behind (slow readers) because we all read at different speeds.

The second challenge is how to keep everyone interested while the novel-sharing proceeds. Fortunately, there are plenty of activities that can work well. The aim is always to encourage children to think more carefully about their reading.

 Whatever the shared novel is, don't forget to have copies of similar books, and others by the same author, available for readers to move on to independently.

The following six activities can be adapted to work with most novels at most ages:

1   Work together to make a group or class timeline showing events in the novel. If (as in *Wuthering Heights*, *Rebecca* or Michael Morpurgo's *Billy the Kid*) there are time shifts and flashbacks, this can really help with the understanding of the plot. Build it up on the classroom wall as you go along.

2   Make a frieze of characters for the classroom wall. Give each pupil responsibility for at least one drawing, painting and so on and for cutting out a character.

3   Encourage pupils to work in pairs to discuss and suggest how the novel might end.

4   Ask one pupil to pretend to take on the role of one of the characters from the novel. S/he talks to the group about his/her thoughts, character, actions, family and so on. Other pupils have to guess who s/he is.

5   Let pupils write a letter from one character to another.

6   Make up orally, or write, a story with the same setting (place and/or time). For example, a riverbank story if you are reading *The Wind in the Willows* or a seventeenth-century story if you are sharing Sally Gardner's *I, Coriander*.

Application

Independent reading in class

Since reading underpins all other learning, there can be few more important classroom activities. Yet time for learners to read independently – while the teacher and classroom assistants read too to reinforce that reading really matters – has been slowly eroded.

In the past, the activity has been given witty acronymic names such as USSR (Uninterrupted Sustained Silent Reading) or ERIC (Everyone Reads in Class).

Now, too many teachers are pressurized into seeing independent reading as a cop-out – perhaps because it is something that they and the pupils might really enjoy together!

If you, or anyone senior to you, needs a justification for silent reading in class, consider these points:

- Because reading is private and individual it allows choice – which pupils rarely get in school.
- It is a fine form of differentiated learning because, perhaps with a bit of guidance, each individual chooses what s/he is capable of reading.
- It gives the teacher a chance to model good practice by reading for 20 minutes or more.
- It creates an opportunity for the teacher to discuss reading with individual students.
- It is a good opportunity for formative assessment.

Remember, *never* set your learners to read while you do something else, such as marking. It gives the impression that reading is a childish thing which you have outgrown now that you have important, adult responsibilities.

Nothing Matters More than Reading (NMMR)! Put it on the classroom wall.

As a way of consolidating the value of Uninterrupted Sustained Silent Reading, ask pupils to keep a reading log, and keep one yourself.

- Use a ring binder.
- Personalize it by covering or decorating it in a way which is relevant to the books the 'logger' likes or has read.
- List the books read with a short review or comment on each. Date these.
- Include a list of books to be read – recommended by a friend, perhaps, or seen reviewed in magazines and so on.
- Some pupils might like to include a picture-based response, such as a mind map or a drawing, to some or all of the books read.

Make sure you:

- find time to discuss each pupil's reading log with him or her
- show and talk about your own log from time to time.

Application

21

Boys

Most practitioners working in education know that it is usually more difficult to persuade boys to read than girls. And there's a lot of research evidence to prove it. In the UK, test results for English at ages 11 and 14, for example, always show that girls are, on average, several percentage points better than boys.

There are a number of reasons for this:

- Until the age of about 16, boys are a few months behind girls of the same age in terms of physical and mental development. Some boys get left behind in literacy even before the age of 11 as the girls forge ahead.

- All children should be physically active, of course, and opportunities must be equal, but there is a slight tendency for boys to be more physically active than girls. (Perhaps this dates back to young cavemen going out hunting while the girls stayed behind?) This means in some cases that the boys find it more difficult to sit still and concentrate.

- Fewer adult men read for pleasure than adult women – especially fiction – so some boys do not see male role models (fathers, grandfathers, uncles) reading at home. And sometimes, there is, anyway, no man at home.

- Only about 20 per cent of primary school teachers are male, so young boys don't see much male reading behaviour at school either.

- Some boys are turned off by fiction which they regard (perhaps influenced by the non-reading males in their lives) as soppy and girlish.

- There is a shortage of high-quality non-fiction on the market to offer boys instead.

Of course, all the above is a generalization. Some boys read fiction just as keenly as their female contemporaries.

Here are a few things to bear in mind as you try to engage boys in reading fiction:

- Some male authors are now deliberately writing fiction books with boy-appeal. Anthony Horowitz's Alex Rider books (now being made into films such as *Stormbreaker*) are good examples. So are most of Alan Gibbons' books.

- Boys do not, in general, want to read books in which the main characters are girls.

- They are put off by anything with a girl's name on the cover – especially if the cover is pink! (These are published in large numbers, however, because profit-hungry publishers know that they will sell – to girls.)

- Boys are often happy to read magazines instead of books. Don't dismiss the fiction they include.

- Even if it means a bit of stereotyping, look for books with boy-friendly settings such as Mal Peet's *Penalty*, which has football in Brazil as its background, or Geraldine McCaughrean's *Kite Rider*, which is about a circus boy in thirteenth-century China.

If you are female, you need to find male role-model readers. Can you swap classes with a male colleague occasionally for reading activities? Consider inviting external male readers into school to talk to pupils about reading habits and favourite books.

Application

Books on film

Many children's books have been made into excellent films for the cinema or television and are now available as DVDs (or videos), for example *The Chronicles of Narnia*, *The Railway Children*, *101 Dalmatians*, *Mary Poppins*, *The Worst Witch*, *Watership Down*, *Charlotte's Web*, *Goodnight Mister Tom*, *Charlie and the Chocolate Factory* – and many others.

So too have many books for teenagers and young adults. At the time of writing, Philip Pullman's *His Dark Materials* is being filmed and the film rights for Jamila Gavin's *Coram Boy* have been sold. And there are plenty of filmed versions of classics, such as stories by Dickens, Conan Doyle, Austen and the Brontës.

Sometimes it helps to show one of these to a group as a way of getting their interest in the characters and story. Then you can introduce them to the book. A youngster who might struggle with a particular book 'cold' will often cope with it easily once s/he has seen a dramatization.

On the other hand, it also makes sense sometimes – with slightly more able readers – to tell them that you will let them see the film as a treat once the group has finished reading the book. Some will then be disappointed with the film which cuts bits out and represents the characters differently from how the reader imagined. If so, you will have made an important point: that reading is usually better!

 The public library is a good place to borrow films from if there is no money in the school budget to buy them.

Try these two classroom ideas for using film adaptations to encourage reading:

- With junior groups, watch Tim Burton's 2005 film of *Charlie and the Chocolate Factory* starring Johnny Depp. Many children will have read the book already, but some won't. Encourage children to choose their favourite scenes from the film and present them to the group. Lead them on to explore all Roald Dahl's other children's titles such as *James and the Giant Peach*, *The Twits* and the Charlie sequel *Charlie and the Great Glass Elevator*. Children who have read these can give oral reviews for the rest of the class.

- Watch one of the many versions of *Pride and Prejudice* together – for groups over age 11. The 2005 film directed by Joe Wright and starring Keira Knightley is fairly authentic and very watchable. Then read aloud some of the novel's key passages – such as the famous opening, or the section in which Darcy finally proposes and is accepted, or one of the funny passages in which Mrs Bennet is being outrageous or Mr Collins obnoxious. If you enthuse enough, some pupils will be encouraged to tackle the book independently – and then there are five other glorious Jane Austen novels to explore.

Application

Stories on CD

Many novels and children's books are now published in a read-aloud form as well as in a print version.

Children's titles range from *Just So Stories* read by Geoffrey Palmer, all the Harry Potter books read by Stephen Fry, Sam West reading *Peter Pan* and Ian McKellan reading Michelle Paver's *Chronicles of Darkness*. Adult authors likely to appeal to teenagers, and whose novels have been recorded as talking books, range from Maeve Binchy and Danielle Steele to Dan Brown, Colin Dexter and Ruth Rendell. Then there are classic novels by Thomas Hardy, Joseph Conrad, Anthony Trollope and the rest.

Some modern titles are read by their authors. Most are the work of skilled, well-known actors.

The availability of an audiobook means that the young people you are trying to encourage to read can – if it suits them – listen to a book rather than read it. And there is nothing wrong with that. It can be a good way into reading for pleasure. And it has the advantage that you can listen while doing something else such as walking to school, sitting on a bus, washing up or tidying your bedroom. All the listener/reader needs is a CD player and these, particularly personal ones, are now very cheap. Some full-length audiobooks are also available to download from sites such as iTunes.

Another advantage to book listening is that it can help to develop and extend a youngster's concentration span. Many twenty-first-century children are so beset with distractions that they really find it quite hard to focus on anything for long. So, any activity which works on this is a bonus.

Enjoying an audiobook also helps to develop listening skills. We live in a very visual world and many children and young people no longer know how to listen and understand well without pictures. A pupil with an improved concentration span and heightened listening ability is much more likely to engage with print books (as well as audiobooks) than one without.

Advice

- Take audiobooks seriously and respect the reading of pupils who use them. Don't regard stories on CDs as a second-class form of reading, and ensure you communicate this attitude to the whole class.

- Stock the classroom and/or school library with a wide range of fiction on CD and encourage learners to borrow them in the same way as printed library books.

- Occasionally, introduce a book to your learners by playing part of a CD reading of it to a group. Or, you could use a computer or electronic white board.

- Invest in as many personal CD players and batteries as the school can run to. Encourage children to use these in the classroom at odd moments – or during independent reading sessions – to listen to story CDs. (You may need to mark the players or otherwise protect them against theft.)

- Listen to fiction on CD yourself and let your learners see you engrossed in your aural 'book', for example as you walk into school or in the school grounds at break time.

Application

2

Non-fiction

Non-fiction: a Cinderella zone

Non-fiction is anything in prose which doesn't tell a made-up story. And it tends, like Cinderella, to get left behind and forgotten while fiction and other forms of children's writing go to the ball.

This is a great pity because some children – especially boys – don't get on with fiction, but can be converted to the reading habit through good, entertaining non-fiction on subjects which grab them. Many a small boy will read anything he can lay his hands on about dinosaurs, for example.

Sometimes the line between fiction and non-fiction becomes rather blurred anyway. In *Pirates, Plants and Plunder!* (Eden Books), Stewart Ross tells half-invented, action-packed, fact-based stories about historical people connected with plants. It is an ingenious idea which results in a set of spiky tales. Or what about Rosemary Sutcliff's Roman novels reissued by OUP in 2007, or Elizabeth Laird's newer *Oranges in No Man's Land* (Macmillan)? Both are fiction, but, from a non-fiction point of view, they are splendid information sources about Roman Britain and war-torn 1980s Beirut respectively.

Our Island Story is another example. It was a book of stories from British history – the Battle of Hastings, the execution of Charles I, Trafalgar, and so on – by H.E. Marshall, first published in 1905. It inspired thousands of school children and endowed them with a love of history, but eventually it fell out of favour. When it was republished in 2005 by Galore Park, *Our Island Story* became a runaway bestseller again.

Advice

Books that impart facts – either through stories or more directly – are another good way of developing reading skills. We need plenty of good non-fiction books in classrooms and libraries.

Encourage children to read non-fiction books, not just as points of reference when they want to know something specific, but as 'reading texts' to be carried around and enjoyed. One pupil might read, for instance, a book which ties in with a television wildlife documentary series while sitting next to another who is absorbed in a novel.

Make sure that you role-model reading non-fiction too. Be seen with biographies, books on history, science, travel and anything else which interests you. Chat to pupils about your choices and your responses to the books.

For the pupil who isn't fictionally inclined, make sure there are plenty of non-fiction books, on a wide range of subjects, available in the classroom and/or library.

Try to create a culture in which everyone in your teaching group(s) – including you – reads as widely as possible from both fiction and non-fiction books.

Application

Balancing words and pictures

Many information books for young readers are little more than picture books with captions. These have a place, of course, but once children reach age seven or eight and beyond, such books are not ideal for building up that all-important reading stamina and might not provide all the information they seek.

So, you need to find non-fiction books which include something meaty to read as well as being well illustrated. Keep it in proportion though. When you read, say, a history book – or pick it up to decide whether you want to read it – what do you look at first? Almost certainly the photographs. Children are no different.

Naturally, the youngest children need more pictures and less writing. Nicholas Allan's witty *Where Willy Went*, published in 2004 by Red Fox, and which teaches the basics of sex education for under-sevens, is an outstanding example of getting the balance right for beginner readers. The skill is to manage the transition and ease them on to an increasing amount of text as their reading ability builds.

Develop the habit of running a mental word count when you look at a page. If you want children to develop their reading you need at least 150 to 250 words per page for reasonably competent readers under 11. As they progress through secondary school, most readers will gradually learn to cope with a balance tilting towards more text and less illustration.

Browse in bookshops and use the 'search inside' facility offered by some internet booksellers to find other books that provide interesting information, accessibly expressed.

 Pictures can add to and clarify meaning and make a book visually more attractive. But words usually matter more!

For 7–14 year olds, *The Young Oxford Encyclopedia of Science* (edited by Richard Dawkins and Robin Kerrod), if you have a copy, is a good example of an information book which has plenty of meaty text to read but is also very well illustrated. With its upbeat accounts of, for instance, meteorites, nuclear energy, telephones and genetics even a non-bookish boy is likely to find it attractive to refer to or browse through. A similar excellent choice is *The Kingfisher Science Encyclopedia*.

Another good example is the well-illustrated *Whitaker's World of Facts* edited by Russell Ash (A&C Black). There is a fact in every sentence of this thematic (rather than alphabetical) and eclectic encyclopedia. In the chapter on building and structure, for example, a double-page spread is devoted to bridges and tunnels. We learn, for instance, that the Golden Gate Bridge in San Francisco was the world's longest for many years after it was built in 1937. Today the longest is the Akashi Kaikyo Bridge in Japan. The page also tells you about very old bridges such as Ironbridge in Shropshire in the UK (1781) and the Bridge of Sighs in Venice (1560). The Language and Literature chapter has a good page on the world's different alphabets, as well as on Braille – and lots more beside.

Display these, and other books like them, in your class or school library and draw attention to them.

Application

Non-fiction at different ages

Early readers

Even the youngest children can be encouraged to be interested in reading through non-fiction books. Take, for example, Nicola Davies's splendid 2005 book *Poo: a Natural History of the Unmentionable* (Walker Books). It is a fascinating exploration of the function of excrement in the animal kingdom, and most children love it because of its 'gross' subject matter and offbeat approach. A mini-edition came out in 2006.

Nicola Davies has herself campaigned widely for non-fiction to be given higher status as part of children's reading. She has written many other fascinating books for young children, such as *Oceans and Seas* and *Extreme Animals*.

Juniors

Slightly older children may like David Orme's dramatic *Tornadoes* in Book House's *What on Earth?* series. There are many excellent books available for juniors, especially on art and how to create it; horses, space, animals; and music and how to make it. And Sam and Susan Stern have written some sparky titles about food, nutrition, health and cookery.

12+

Over 12s are often happy dipping into adult non-fiction books, but, if they don't seem to be, a trawl through the Hobbies and Interests section under Children's Books on Amazon, for example, will suggest plenty of titles, topics and authors.

Advice

Whatever the age and reading level of the young people you are working with, involve them in helping to choose non-fiction books to buy for the school. Look at print or online catalogues with them. Talk about the non-fiction books they already read and those that they would like to read – perhaps more by the same author or publisher or on the same topic. Ask them too about 'new' topics they would like to read about.

Some titles will, of course, be related to the curriculum, but don't be afraid to go outside it. The very best reason for wanting to read a non-fiction book is because it is about something which interests you. Any reading helps to build reading skills and establish the reading habit.

The following list is by no means exhaustive, but – in addition to the authors mentioned opposite – these writers have written many fine non-fiction books for under-14s on a wide range of subjects and in a variety of formats, and will give you a good starting point.

- Nick Arnold
- Steve Bloom
- Andrew Langley
- Kathryn Senior
- Philip Steele
- Carole Stott
- Fiona Watt
- Angela Wilkes.

Generally good series to take a look at include:

- Kingfisher's *I Wonder Why*
- Dorling Kindersley's *Eyewitness Guides*
- OUP's *Would You Believe...*

Building on children's interests

If you want to encourage children to read non-fiction, you need to know what they are interested in. Sometimes, a child who is otherwise turned off by reading will avidly consume anything written about a pet subject. It can be an ideal starting point for a reluctant reader.

In a London comprehensive school, I once taught a boy who was in love with buses. I think he knew every bus route in London. It was certainly easier to ask him about a journey than to look at a timetable. Although bright, he wasn't a keen reader, but would read anything concerned with buses – so that was a way into reading for him. (And when he left school he took an administrative job with what was then London Transport, where I'm sure he was a great asset!)

It is worth trying to build chatty relationships with your learners so that you know what they are interested in. If you teach large numbers this isn't always easy, so train your teaching assistants to do the same. Then, as a team, you stand a good chance of knowing the special points of appeal of each learner.

And learners' interests are not always predictable. As well as my young friend's fascination with London buses, I have worked with children captivated by equally unlikely topics, such as Marilyn Monroe, sharks, English folk dancing, bull terriers, black and white films, and the life and times of Charles Dickens.

Once you have the information, you can make sure there are plenty of books available on these topics. It's another take on 'start where the pupil is at'.

Advice

Devote a lesson or two to telling each other about your special interests.

Start by telling the group about one of two of yours. Be as offbeat and specific as you can. If it were me, I might talk about personal passions such as donkeys, Shakespeare plays, irises or Pre-Raphaelite paintings. Books are available on all of these (and almost certainly any other topic you can think of) and I have read large numbers. Show pupils a few books relevant to your special interests.

Then encourage members of the group to say what their special interests are. This is a good speaking and listening activity in its own right. It is also an excellent way of 'researching' children's potential reading topics. Make an unobtrusive note of the subjects they pick.

Afterwards, you might invite the child who is wild about aircraft, or toads, to help you choose some suitable books on the subject for the school library. Involve as many pupils as you can.

Later, another speaking and listening lesson could include children talking to the group about the non-fiction books they helped to order and have now read – to encourage others to read them too.

You can try this with learners of almost any age from about six or seven upwards.

Biography and autobiography

Many children and young people like reading life stories, whether they are written by the subject or by someone else.

Young readers

There are a number of good biographical series available, such as Hodder Wayland's *Scientists*, which includes books on Graham Bell, Da Vinci and Einstein, and Heinemann Library's *Writers Uncovered*, which has books on Jacqueline Wilson and Terry Pratchett, as well as *Famous Lives*, which features people like Shakespeare and Ho Chi Minh.

Another good example is the small but growing series of biographies for 7–11 year olds published by Dorling Kindersley. It includes titles on Helen Keller, Diana, Princess of Wales, Mandela and Gandhi – so there is much multicultural interest and history here. And the books, although pleasingly illustrated, include whole pages of text.

Many quite young children have enjoyed Roald Dahl's books about his childhood: *Boy* and *Going Solo* (Puffin). They also like *War Boy: A Wartime Childhood* by Michael Foreman (Pavilion), partly because his illustrations are so familiar.

Readers who enjoy Michael Morpurgo's many novels and stories might like to discover more about him through *Dear Mr Morpingo: Inside the World of Michael Morpurgo* by Geoff Fox (Wizard Books).

Older readers

Anne Frank: The Diary of a Young Girl (Penguin) is probably one of the most remarkable autobiographical books ever written.

Many older students like to read horrifying stories of terrible childhoods, such as *Angela's Ashes* by Frank McCourt (HarperPerennial) or *A Child Called 'It'* by Dave Pelzer (Orion).

It also worth encouraging older students to read Bill Bryson's thoughtful and witty books. His autobiographical *The Life and Times of the Thunderbolt Kid* (Black Swan) is one of his best.

If you talk to young people about biography and autobiography, many will tell you that they like reading about sports personalities. Make the most of this enthusiasm.

Some of these are biography and some are autobiography (although the latter are often actually written by a professional known as a 'ghost writer').

Some will be about sporting legends of the past such as W.G. Grace and Bobby Moore. Others are about, or by, more recent or current sports achievers such as Wayne Rooney, Kelly Holmes and Andy Murray.

Sport biography is a popular genre with readers of all ages. Any bookshop (high street or internet) will have a large selection.

Teenagers will often read sport books intended for adults if they are drawn to the subject. Biographical writing is usually quite accessible.

It is more difficult to find good sport biographies for younger readers. Nonetheless, you can help children to read sections of the books meant for older readers and/or read sections aloud to them.

Another possible activity is to get the pupils to write their own short biography of their sporting heroes. Then they can swap them for reading, which can be a real spur to read more.

The children, and you, should browse regularly in the biography section of the school (and possibly public) library. Study the biography areas of websites about books too.

Books about animals

Reading about animals appeals to many children. The books tend to fall into two camps – anthropomorphic, in which the animals are given human characteristics and behave like people, and 'straight' in which animals are, well, animals.

Many animal stories are fiction with a non-fiction message. Consider Eric Carle's famous *The Very Hungry Caterpillar* for the youngest children. Carle's story stretches a point about exactly what a caterpillar might eat, but it also teaches three things: the days of the week, that caterpillars have to eat a lot and that caterpillars turn into butterflies. So it isn't just fiction.

Richard Adams' whimsical *Watership Down*, with its epic tale of rabbits, is highly anthropomorphic and, like *The Wind in the Willows*, encouraged others writers to use similar techniques for other animals. William Horwood, for example, wrote novels about moles – beginning with *Duncton Wood*. Such books always teach a lot about the life, history, behaviour and habits of the animal in question.

As they edge towards 10 or 11 years old, however, most readers prefer 'straight' non-fiction books if they are looking for insights into animal behaviour. Those by Gerald Durrell, James Herriot and David Taylor, for example, have stood the test of time and are funny as well as informative. J. H. Williams' books about his dealings with elephants in Burma in the 1930s and 1940s, especially *Elephant Bill*, fascinate some young readers too. Steve Irwin wrote extensively and entertainingly about his work with crocodiles.

Information books that accompany television wildlife series such as the BBC's *Planet Earth*, or anything else by David Attenborough, are an excellent source of non-fiction about animals. So are Jane Goodall's books about apes, such as *My Life With the Chimpanzees* (Aladdin) and *Gorillas in the Mist* by Dian Fossey (Phoenix).

If you like to read about animals, talk to your learners about your choices and what you have discovered. Remarks on the lines of, 'Did you know that... a polar bear's skin is black... a rabbit's teeth keep growing throughout its life... a duck-billed platypus has poison glands?' go down well. Share the details of where you found this information and enthuse about the book.

You can use film to stimulate interest too. Show a class the 1979 film of *Tarka the Otter* beautifully narrated by Peter Ustinov (issued on DVD in 2006). Talk to the children afterwards about otters and draw from them all the 'natural history' information which is embedded in the film. Even quite young children will be able to do this with help. Then encourage them to read Henry Williamson's book (or sections of it if they are very young) on which it is based. Later they might read *Ring of Bright Water* by Gavin Maxwell which is also about otters (and was also made into a film).

Similarly, you could watch an episode of the BBC's *Planet Earth*, for example, to promote reading about topics of interest covered in the programme.

Anyone who enjoys fiction, and is interested in reading about animals, might be steered towards fiction-with-information books by Brian Jacques, Dick King-Smith, Dodie Smith, Paul Gallico, Derek Tangye and many others.

Application

History books

There are many youngster-friendly books available on the Romans, Tudors and Victorians (because they feature prominently in the primary curriculum in the UK) and on the twentieth-century dictators who dominate the history curriculum in secondary schools.

So – if the aim is to promote eclectic reading for pleasure and development – it is worthwhile leading young readers towards other aspects of history too. Some will be keen to read and learn more only about what they have studied in lessons – and there's nothing wrong with that. Make sure though that there are plenty of 'real' books as opposed to just textbooks available.

For wider reading, look for attractive books about, for instance, the English and American civil wars, the Boxer rebellion in China, the rise and fall of Napoleon, the Black Death. Much of what happened in history was dramatic and children are quite easily engaged by it.

As with wildlife, television tie-in books by authors such as David Starkey, Simon Schama, Richard Holmes, Michael Wood and Bettany Hughes often appeal.

Historical fiction

Don't overlook historical novels. They are billed as fiction, but aren't – quite. Mal Peet's *The Penalty* (Walker Books) is set partly in the seventeenth century when African slaves were being taken to South America by the Spanish. It is a history book as well as a novel. So is *King of Shadows* by Susan Cooper (Puffin), which tells of an American boy who comes to London to take part in a drama project at the Globe Theatre – but he gets shifted into Tudor England. Gripping novel as it is, it is also an account of London life in Elizabethan times. Both books are suitable for readers aged 12 and over.

Teenage readers who enjoy historical fiction will probably like adult books by Sarah Dunant, Philippa Gregory and Tracy Chevalier. Victoria Hislop's novel *The Island* (Headline) is about leprosy in Crete in the 1930s and 1940s. It is an entertaining source of information and easy to read.

Advice

Bear in mind a few dos and don'ts when you're trying to encourage young readers to read history books.

Do:

- be aware that young readers like narrative, so the stories implicit in historical events work well
- value historical novels
- read history yourself and 'sell' it to your learners
- stock up with books which go beyond the curriculum
- encourage even very young children to read books with a historical purpose
- make it clear to older children that history is why we are what we are now.

Don't:

- expect young readers necessarily to read a history book right through
- forget that different aspects or periods of history appeal to different people for different reasons
- suggest – ever – that history is boring or irrelevant.

Reading about places

Young readers

Children, like adults, can sometimes be persuaded to read non-fiction books about places they have visited, places they would like to go to and places they just want to dream about – call it armchair travel, if you like. It is another useful way of reinforcing reading skills.

Remember when you are looking for youngster-friendly travel books that they don't have to be about anywhere exotic. Experience of place starts as soon as you step across your own doorstep, after all.

That's why books such as James Mayhew's *Katie in London* (Orchard) and *The Story of London* by Richard Brassey (Orion) appeal even to readers living in the south of England. There can be something comforting and comfortable in reading about places you already know quite well. For young readers elsewhere in the UK and abroad who don't know London, reading about it is a good place to start.

Younger readers wanting to explore more exotic places might like *Babar's World Tour* by Laurent de Brunhoff (Abrams).

Older readers

For older learners, especially those a bit reluctant to turn to books, don't forget travel articles in newspapers and magazines. Weekend newspapers in particular give considerable space to travel features. Cutting them out and taking them to school – perhaps to put on a regularly changed noticeboard, and encouraging children to do the same, can promote reading as well as interest in other parts of the country or world.

Older readers might also like browsing in travel guides such as those from Lonely Planet or Rough Guides. There is no reason why some of these shouldn't be in the school library.

Make sure the library is stocked with travel writing by authors such as Chris Stewart (Spain), Peter Mayle (France), Frances Mayes (Italy) and Michael Palin (everywhere), so that there are plenty of 'place' books for secondary students to choose from.

Advice

Barnaby Bear is a registered trademark of the Geographical Association (geography.org). Barnaby's purpose is to teach five–seven year olds about the world, and he has spawned an extensive range of books and DVDs as well as a BBC television series.

There is a wide range of Barnaby Bear 'big books' for classroom use and ordinary 'little' books for use by individuals or groups.

Many young children enjoy titles in the Where in the World is Barnaby Bear? series. It includes:

- *Barnaby Bear goes to Brittany*
- *Barnaby Bear goes to Dublin*
- *Barnaby Bear goes to Norway*
- *Barnaby Bear goes to Kenya.*

Get to know Barnaby Bear and introduce him to your pupils. He is normally presented as a way of teaching geography, but he also has the potential to encourage reading. There is a dedicated Barnaby Bear website at barnabybear.co.uk

Reading around the subject at secondary level

When subjects are rigidly separated into different time slots and everything that a student needs to pass (most) exams is specified in detail, it is easy to lose sight of subject-related, wider reading – an activity which used to be called 'reading around the subject'.

It meant that if you were studying RE at GCSE or O level you might be encouraged to read Richard Dawkins' *The God Delusion* (Black Swan). Or, if you were doing GCSE PE, you might read biographies of sportspeople who excel (or excelled) in a game or activity you like. Similarly, geography students were encouraged to read *National Geographic* magazine, drama students *The Stage*, and economics students *The Economist* – all many years before leaving school.

There are plenty of novels which could, if allowed to under the curriculum, be providing factual information too. Mal Peet's *The Penalty* (Walker Books) is strong on the climate, crime and ambience of South America. So is Eva Ibbotson's *Journey to the River Sea* (Macmillan) – with a nineteenth-century twist. Anyone who reads the teenage novel *Angel Blood* by John Singleton (Ladybird) will learn much to inform ethics discussions in science; and Melvyn Burgess's *Junk* (Puffin) would be a good PSHE recommendation. And these are just examples.

Sadly the curriculum has narrowed. There is now such focus on learning precisely what is needed for exams that few students get much breadth from wider reading these days. Instead, lessons are beset with that heart-sinking question, 'Do we need this for the exam, Miss?'

This is a great pity, and teachers would do well to try to bring back reading around the subject as a normal part of school life. Apart from the advantage it brings in widening subject knowledge, it is yet another opportunity to promote reading.

Here are some suggestions for promoting reading around the subject in secondary classes:

- Construct lists of books and publications which relate to your subject – however peripherally. Put them on the wall, on the intranet and give students printed copies. Update the lists regularly.

- Have a mini-library of subject-related books in your teaching room – available to be borrowed by the students.

- Most young secondary readers (especially girls) are still enjoying stories, so think laterally about novels which could have a bearing on your subject. For example, *Girl With a Pearl Earring* by Tracy Chevalier (HarperCollins) for history of art, Clare Clark's *The Great Stink* (Penguin) for history, Geraldine McCaughrean's *Stop the Train* (OUP) for geography, and so on.

- Read and recommend biographies of practitioners of your subject – great mathematicians, scientists, designers, artists, musicians, politicians and so on.

- Subscribe to subject-related magazines and make them available in the teaching room. Read them yourself and draw attention to particularly interesting articles.

- Use a whole lesson, occasionally, to talk about wider reading in your subject. Tell your students about what you have been reading yourself so that you model good reading behaviour. Make recommendations. Ask your students for suggestions.

- Put a large notice or banner on the wall which says something like 'Reading around the subject makes you more knowledgeable – read more books about biology'.

3

Reading for information

Reference books

A lot of the information we want comes from the internet these days, and we shall turn to that shortly. But encyclopedias, dictionaries and other printed reference books are still very useful.

A book on the desk, or close by, is often a quicker source of information than laboriously working through a search engine. It is almost certainly more reliable too than some internet sites.

If I want, for example, the dates of a British king, I always turn to my one-volume *Hutchinson Encyclopedia*. If I want a spelling or meaning, I use the *Collins English Dictionary*, which sits within inches of my keyboard. If I want to know the origin of an expression, phrase or what some idiomatic oddity means, *Brewer's Dictionary of Phrase & Fable* is nearby.

Another handy little volume is *Pears Cyclopaedia*. Like the perennial *Whitaker's Almanack*, it is laid out thematically rather than alphabetically. Both are full of useful, annually updated information which is speedily accessible.

Young people need to be made aware of what is available and what they can find out from each book. And, in practice, these sorts of books are so interesting that as soon as you look up one thing you find yourself distracted because something else catches your eye and you read that too. Encourage this 'go where it takes you' approach to reference books. It might slow up the progress of the project in hand, but it is helping to develop high-level reading behaviour.

Advice

Growing up in a multimedia world, learners also build up reading ability as they search for digital information or browse in newspapers and magazines. We should encourage it.

A good example of how you can excite secondary school students and get them to read more reference material is the long and well-established Companion series published by Oxford University Press (see oup.co.uk/reference/companions).

The Oxford Companion to English Literature, *The Oxford Companion to Music* and a few others have been around since before the Second World War and have been updated and reworked by new editors many times. Others have been compiled for the first time only recently.

The Oxford Companion to English Literature, first published in 1932, appeared in its latest version – edited by Margaret Drabble – in 2006. Book titles, names of authors spanning a thousand years, characters in books and book-related topics are presented in alphabetical order. If a student wants a potted biography of Charles Dickens or a résumé of *Bleak House*, or is wondering who Uriah Heep was, this is the place to look. Put it in the school library and have as many copies as possible in reading-aware classrooms. Show the students how to use it and let them see you using it too.

At the time of writing, there are 56 titles in the Oxford Companion series, including *The Oxford Companion to World Mythology*, and *Shakespeare*, *Jazz*, *Food* and *Ships and the Sea*.

Some of the guides are also produced in 'concise' versions, which you might find more suitable for younger and less confident readers. *The Concise Oxford Companion to English Literature*, for instance, was published in 2003.

Application

Newspapers

Don't underestimate the worth of newspapers. They are an invaluable source of information about politics, national and international events, science, discoveries, sport, the arts, health and, especially at weekends, many other topics. Newspapers really should be part of every youngster's daily reading habits.

In the UK there is a long tradition of newspaper reading and more newspapers are published here than in most other countries. It is a missed opportunity if young people don't acquire the habit.

Unfortunately, fewer than 50 per cent of UK households ever buy a newspaper and the figure is even lower in many other countries. Therefore, many pupils come to school with little or no experience of newspapers and they are not used to seeing adults reading them.

In which case, there should be plenty of newspapers available in school. Shop around to see if you can get a good deal. Some of the newspaper publishers are so keen to hook young readers that they will sometimes subsidize newspapers in schools. Or, you could ask your local newsagent to give you a cut-price offer if you buy several papers each day. Take your own newspaper to school with you and ask colleagues to do the same.

Try to rise above newspaper snobbery and let the students read at their own level. Every paper is informative in some way and helps to build up reading stamina – even if it also has lots of photographs and is stronger on celebrity gossip than hard news. It really doesn't matter whether little Jemina chooses the *Daily Mail* or *USA Today* over *The Times* or *Washington Post*. Many readers will anyway start with an easy-read, accessible paper and move on to something more challenging as they get older or when they feel ready. Don't push it. Just encourage newspaper reading in general and chat to the children about articles you and they have read in newspapers.

Younger readers, or those who really find large, adult newspapers off-putting, should try *Newsademic* (newsademic.com). It is a fortnightly, international newspaper written in accessible language, but dealing with some quite challenging topics – such as wars and elections – alongside scientific discoveries and quirky things which happen across the world. It is aimed at 9–16 year olds.

It is sold on subscription and delivered on alternate Fridays by email as a PDF which you can then print. For different fees, you can subscribe to the paper or, if you want to put it on your school's intranet, buy a licence.

Newsademic has been going since 2005 and subscribers can access all the past issues on a searchable database on the website.

Classroom activities are an optional extra to encourage the students to read more closely. If you buy those, they too arrive on alternate Fridays. There is plenty of interesting reading for the independent student, as well as useful cross-curricular links with geography, science, history, citizenship and so on.

You can download a free sample issue from *Newsademic*'s website.

You might also like to browse the *Newspaper* (thenewspaper.org.uk), written for children of eight and over. However, it is issued only half-termly, so be aware that the 'news' might not be very up to date.

Magazines

There is at least one specialist magazine for just about every specialism you can think of – and many more you probably can't! Look through the magazine listings in *Writers' & Artists' Yearbook* or *The Writers' Handbook* (both in the reference section of most public libraries) for a sense of the range. And/or take half an hour to browse the stock in a big newsagent's.

Sometimes, reluctant readers – especially boys – can be persuaded to read quite substantial articles in magazines devoted to subjects which really interest them. When I was a young teacher in charge of a school library in a 'tough' boys' school in London, I found I could coax dozens of boys – who wouldn't have dreamed of picking up a book – to read the *Angling Times*. Non-readers they certainly weren't. They soaked up complex articles about fishing like blotting paper. It was a real boost to literacy and the status of reading in that school.

Football titles are another obvious theme, along with anything relating to other sports. Many pupils are interested in technology, films, various sorts of craft, and the environment. It makes good sense to chat to pupils about which titles they would like to see in school.

Meaty current affairs magazines such as *The Economist*, *The Spectator*, *New Statesman* or *New Internationalist* may appeal to older students in a secondary school.

Buying large numbers of magazines is expensive, of course. But back copies can often be collected free. Find out what your colleagues buy regularly or subscribe to. They may be willing to give you magazines they have finished with. Similarly, parents might be able to help. Talk to your newsagent too. Unsold magazines are usually returned to the supplier, but you may be able to persuade your friendly newsagent to save a few for your school.

To take just one topic, drama and the performing arts are a passion for many young people. In England, a growing number of specialist schools are taking performing arts as their main specialism – over 200 at the time of writing.

The Stage, a weekly magazine founded in the late nineteenth century and devoted to the performing arts, is a good example of a specialist publication which can encourage reading among enthusiasts.

It includes news about the industry – venues opening and closing, new productions, funding arrangements and arguments. There are features about performers, reviews of productions, information about education and a section about backstage work – among other things. It is widely read by almost everyone working in – or wanting to work in – performing arts.

Young drama buffs tend to be so passionate about the performing arts that they will live, breathe and eat them if they get the chance. So harness that passion to help young people develop the reading habit. Have copies of *The Stage* in the classroom or library. Read it yourself and lead your pupils to it. Some will have ambitions to work in the performing arts and be hungry for information about the industry.

It is cheaper to subscribe to *The Stage* than to buy it weekly. Some of its content is available free online at thestage.co.uk

Internet: general

When the internet first began to develop in the early 1990s (odd to reflect just how young it still is), people said that it would kill reading. In fact, the opposite is the case. Because nearly everything on the internet has to be read – using all the traditional reading techniques – it actually promotes reading.

It just means that most of us now turn to the internet for the sort of practical information – railway timetables, phone numbers or street maps for example – which we would once have looked for in printed directories or books.

No teacher is King Canute. We cannot hold back this technological tide. Anyway, why should we want to? The internet is, effectively, a bigger and more efficient (though not always accurate) encyclopedia than any of us could accommodate in our classrooms or homes. It also comes with the sort of information – such as the latest news – that you would not find in a conventional encyclopedia.

So – although we all know that it is books which make the most difference to learners' overall achievement – encourage them to make the most of the internet too. Every time they click into a search engine they are reading, so the internet has a part to play in reading development.

 Computer games are a different matter. Most use little or no language. Some may develop skills useful in other subjects, but, from a reading point of view, they are generally useless – the equivalent of junk food.

Introduce your pupils to bbc.co.uk. An electronic whiteboard would be an ideal way to do this, if you have access to one, because then you can work with a group rather than an individual or pair.

The news section of the site is excellent and covers a wide range of areas:

- World
- UK
- Northern Ireland
- Scotland
- Wales
- Business
- Politics
- Health
- Education
- Science/Nature
- Technology
- Entertainment.

There are captioned photographs, maps and diagrams to make the meaning of the news stories clear. So this is a good source of reading for all children from age about seven upwards.

The pages are uncluttered by advertising, and the latest headlines continually loop across the top of the news home page.

There are also links to a magazine section and special reports and to sports news, Newsround and the historical On this day.

 One good way of encouraging pupils to read carefully from this site, and to learn their way around it, would be to set key questions and challenge them to find the answers.

Internet: education

Another way of using the internet to develop reading is to lead children to sites offering quite substantial blocks of written text and give them time and space to read them.

If, for instance, an eight year old is learning about Ancient Egypt s/he would find the information at ancientegypt.co.uk interesting and worthwhile – it is part of the British Museum's education work. There is plenty there to read and the illustrations and photographs are excellent.

Similarly, a ten year old wanting information about animal conservation across the world will find good reading material on the World Wildlife Fund's website, wwf.org.uk

We need to remember, however, that some people – irrespective of age or reading competence – find reading from a perpendicular screen quite difficult. Be prepared to arrange to print anything a pupil wants to read (or you want him/her to read) if s/he is more comfortable reading horizontally from paper.

On the other hand, print on screen can often be enlarged, or set on a different-coloured background, which can benefit some pupils with reading difficulties who will find it better than reading from white paper.

The following websites might interest your learners, and all have the potential to boost reading stamina:

- The National Trust: nationaltrust.org.uk. The Families and children section of Learning and discovery has excellent reading for young children including facts and fun activities guided by Trusty the Hedgehog. Elsewhere on the site is useful heritage information for secondary students.

- RSPCA: rspca.org.uk has an Animal Action Club online, in the Under 8teenz section. It is linked to the RSPCA's printed magazine *Animal Action* (Another one for the library?), which is aimed at under-13s.

- Save the Children: savethechildren.org.uk is full of good reading about education across the world.

- Ofsted: ofsted.gov.uk. It may interest older students to read what inspectors have said about their own school and other schools known to them.

- Examining bodies: aqa.org.uk, ocr.org.uk, edexcel.org.uk (and others in Wales, Scotland and Northern Ireland). Although aimed at teachers, GCSE and A level students could be encouraged to read the information put out by the people who set and mark their exams.

Application

Internet: books and famous people

Help children to use the internet to find reading matter about famous people past and present, films, plays, music and even books – which takes us back to the basis of reading.

If, for example, children have seen a film and want to know more about its cast, plot, director or how it was made, putting the film title into a search engine will throw up useful websites with plenty to read – especially if it's a well-known or cult film such as *The Lord of the Rings* trilogy, *Charlotte's Web* or *The Wizard of Oz*.

The internet also has a lot of information about famous people from the past on historical and other websites – from Cleopatra and Aristotle to Helen Keller, Martin Luther King, Marilyn Monroe and Douglas Bader – all of whom are likely to arise in curriculum work as well as being topics of general interest. Most young people are more likely to read short life stories online than to pick up a hefty book-length biography – although for some, the former will lead to the latter.

Similarly, if children want, or need, to know about music and musicians, there are plenty of websites to provide good reading material.

If everyone can read comfortably their chosen texts on screen, fine. If not, organize getting it printed.

We want children to read more books. Don't overlook the internet as a valuable source of information about books. It can raise awareness of what's available and promote interest in books – there are plenty of reviews, summaries and synopses by professional writers and by readers of all ages. There is also scope for students to write reviews themselves – and post them on the internet. Try some publishers' websites for this (oup.co.uk and penguin.co.uk are two of the best).

Amazon's website is an excellent index of books. Whether or not you, or a student, wants to buy a book from Amazon, it's a very useful way of finding out what, for instance, an author's latest book is, or what books are available on a particular subject. It also gives you price, ISBN, number of pages and date of publication. Most books have a publisher's synopsis. Many have a review written by a commissioned Amazon reviewer. Often there are reviews posted free by readers too, which pupils might like to contribute to. The new 'search inside' facility available for increasing numbers of titles means you can read a small section of the book on screen as a taster.

Many authors have their own informative and entertaining websites, for example:

- philip-pullman.com
- annefine.co.uk
- malorieblackman.co.uk
- marcussedgwick.com

There are many more. Encourage children to read these for biographical information and updates, as well as synopses of books and news about events.

Finding out more about books from websites could be a useful activity for a library lesson at almost any age. And all the information has to be read, so it improves reading skill.

Application

Leaflets

There is reading material all around us in the leaflets we can pick up almost everywhere we go. Supermarkets have recipe leaflets and pamphlets giving information about healthy eating as well as flyers promoting other company products such as financial services. Health centres and GP surgeries have racks of pamphlets about medical conditions, and hotels, tourist offices and libraries are full of colourful leaflets about local places to visit. And those are just a few examples!

Use such leaflets as a free educational resource. On the whole, they are written in accessible language because they are designed for mass consumption. But they all use words; sometimes quite a lot of words. Many are aimed directly at younger readers or are about topics likely to interest young people (health, films, the environment and so on) which therefore encourage them to read.

A lot of important everyday information is produced in leaflets, manuals and forms. They are therefore essential reading for adults. So it is a good idea to work on them with children as part of their reading.

It is worth gathering up a selection wherever you go and taking them into school. You can also encourage children to pick up and bring some into school and share with others what is interesting about what they have read. It helps to reinforce the concept that all reading is important.

In a primary school classroom, keep a box or basket for collected leaflets so that a child who, for whatever reason, is not reading a book can pick up a leaflet and read it in odd moments.

You can design a good English lesson around leaflets in order to explore the use of language for different purposes and in different forms. The pupils have to read in detail the leaflets they are discussing, so reading development is inbuilt.

A leaflet can:

- give instructions (for example a recipe or set of game rules)
- try to sell you something (a flyer for a supermarket credit card, a take-away menu)
- give advice about medical symptoms ('Don't worry the doctor if these symptoms mean it's just a cold.')
- tell you where to go for help (such as an MP's surgery information leaflet found in the main library)
- inform you about local services (Citizens Advice Bureau details, library facilities and opening times, bus route maps and timetables, recycling provisions)
- encourage you to visit a castle, house, garden or theme park (tourist brochure)

...and many other things.

Teach readers, even when they are quite young, to look critically at:

- sentence and paragraph length
- vocabulary
- style
- tone
- layout (for example, font sizes and colours, bullet points, boxes and so on)
- amount of text compared with illustration.

Then they can answer this question orally or in writing: 'How well does this leaflet do what it sets out to do?'

If there is time in a lesson, encourage learners to compare two or more different leaflets.

Role-modelling

As with fiction, pupils need to see that the grown-ups they respect read anything and everything they can lay their hands on – in an ever widening range of formats – to get information. The maxim 'Do as I say, but not as I do' never works in education (or in any other context for that matter)!

So, don't be afraid to say enthusiastically to a class, small group or individual, 'Last night at home I came across a marvellous new website about Nelson Mandela. It's got lots of information I'd never read before, the graphics are great and it's very easy to use. So have a look at it!' Or, 'Josh, I know how keen you are on stage lighting so I've brought you this article I spotted in *The Stage*. I think there are points in it which will interest you.' Or (to a small group preparing a presentation on animal experimentation), 'Have you looked at the FRAME website? (Fund for the Replacement of Animals in Medical Experiments, frame.org.uk) I stumbled across it the other day and it taught me a lot that I didn't know.'

Let your learners see you looking at magazines and newspapers in the library or, occasionally, in class. At the very least, have a newspaper on your desk or poking out of your bag.

Make sure pupils see you researching information from the internet – not just as a one-off, but regularly.

Model computer-screen reading just as you would book reading.

Set up a classroom wall display called 'Want to know? Where to look'!

Pick some sample interest areas relevant to the age group you are working with. Topics for nine year olds, for instance, might be dinosaurs, J.K. Rowling and France. For 13 year olds they might be The Beatles, spots and pimples, and conservation of the giant panda.

Link each subject label with ribbons, thread or lines to a range of written information sources. Use as many graphics as you can to make the display as visually interesting as possible. Involve the pupils throughout the process.

For example, for *Spots and pimples*, the links could include:

- teenage magazines such as *Sugar*
- leaflets from doctors' surgeries, health centres or pharmacies
- newspaper articles by doctor-journalists such as Thomas Stuttaford in *The Times*
- articles in newspapers which run a lot of health advice such as the *Daily Mail*
- health websites such as netdoctor.co.uk or patient.co.uk

For a topic on France, a poster could look like this:

Leave a space on the display for pupils to list other useful sources that they find themselves.

4

Poems and plays

Poems and plays as reading

Poems and plays can be read silently by individuals just as novels and non-fiction can. Bear in mind, though, many poems need to be read aloud. Similarly, although anyone who is going to take part in a play will first read the script silently and independently – as we expect students to do for English exams – plays are meant to be performed and experienced as performance.

Poems

Children like poetry – old, new, funny, sad, whatever – and can often be persuaded to read a short poem when they would be daunted by a whole book.

Try reading poems aloud when there is a tiny space to fill, such as two minutes at the end of a lesson. Then tell the class where and how to find more poems like that one, for example by the same poet, on the same subject, using the same rhythm or rhyme. There's a lot of poetry on the internet if that is a preferable source to a big daunting anthology.

Plays

Plays, too, are quick and quite easy to read because of the way they are laid out on the page. There are some pupils who would rather (and be better able to) read a play than a novel.

If you read a play with a class or group, take one of the parts yourself. It helps to maintain the momentum of the reading.

Advice

Many children love the rhythm and rhyme of poetry and the structure of plays with their potential for group reading and expression. So, as part of reading development both of these forms are worth focusing on – and not just in English lessons.

Poems and plays can sometimes – rather usefully – point older students back to fiction because so many story writers have been inspired by the work of poets and playwrights, particularly classics. For example:

- *King of Shadows* by Susan Cooper (Puffin) relates to *A Midsummer Night's Dream*.

- *Alone on a Wide Sea* by Michael Morpurgo (HarperCollins) makes reference to Coleridge's 'The Rime of the Ancient Mariner'.

- *Ophelia* by Lisa M. Klein (Bloomsbury) is inspired by *Hamlet*.

- *Troy* by Adèle Geras (Scholastic) retells the *Iliad* from an unusual perspective.

Introduce the students to the play or poem – or extracts – which was in the novelist's mind. Use it as a springboard for the novel. Read a chapter aloud and then have copies for interested students to take away and continue reading.

Alternatively, introduce the novel first. Then share a bit (or all) of the poem or play at the root of it.

For the very youngest children, there are many lovely 'spin off' stories based on nursery rhymes – the first poetry most of us learn. For example:

- *Clever Polly and the Stupid Wolf* by Catherine Storr (Puffin)

- *Each Peach Pear Plum* by Janet and Allan Ahlberg (Puffin)

- *The Jolly Postman or Other People's Letters* by Janet and Allan Ahlberg (Viking).

Application

Exposure to poetry

Most children and young people enjoy poems which tell stories – narrative poetry. There are some very old and famous narrative poems such as the anonymous 'The Ballad of Patrick Spens', along with poems by Wordsworth, Tennyson, Robert Louis Stevenson and many more.

There are also more modern story poems. Take a look at the work of poets like Charles Causley, Wendy Cope, Grace Nicholls and Kit Wright.

Younger children are often most engaged by funny poems. Try Thomas Hood's 'November', Ogden Nash's poems or Edward Lear's limericks, all of which might be new to them. In our own time, Roger McGough, Michael Rosen, Roald Dahl and Colin McNaughton have, among many others, written a great deal of poetry which is often thoughtful as well as funny.

Suggest that pupils read poems to themselves, or to each other in pairs, whenever there is a very short time slot. Keep anthologies handy in the classroom and use a computer to create some home-made wall posters of poems – or buy ready-made ones. You can also use an electronic whiteboard to display a poem. If you are not using the whiteboard for something else, you could have a poem on it like a wall display. Some pupils will certainly read it if it's there. And why not use a poem for your screen saver or desktop background?

You can buy cassettes and CDs of poetry too. Some pupils might like to listen (on headphones) to poems and follow the text in a book at the same time. The website poetryarchive.org is an expanding collection of poets reading their own poems, with accompanying on-screen text which can be read at the same time.

 Don't worry if readers don't know the meaning of every word or don't get 'heavy' about poetry reading. As T.S. Eliot said, 'Genuine poetry can communicate before it is understood.'

Advice

Have a session in the week when all pupils reads poetry of their own choice – not with you 'teaching' it, but for pleasure (and reading development). Let them see you reading poetry with enthusiasm too.

A few suggestions are:

Ages 8–12

- 'The Pied Piper of Hamelin' by Robert Browning
- 'Matilda' by Hilaire Belloc
- 'The Highwayman' by Alfred Noyes
- 'Macavity – The Mystery Cat' by T.S. Eliot
- 'Jabberwocky' by Lewis Carroll
- 'Night Mail' by W.H. Auden

Ages 12+

- 'Snake' by D.H. Lawrence
- 'The Lady of Shalott' by Alfred Tennyson
- 'Ruined' by Thomas Hardy
- 'The Journey of the Magi' by T.S. Eliot
- 'Cowboy Song' by Charles Causley
- 'The Eve of St Agnes' by John Keats

The Dragon Book of Verse (OUP) is a useful tried-and-tested anthology, and there is a good selection of well-known poetry which you and/or your pupils can download free from poems-online.org

Raising the status of poetry

Poetry tends to get marginalized as reading matter. Of all the books sold or borrowed from libraries only a tiny percentage is poetry.

Some adults say this is because poetry is difficult, inaccessible, elitist, pretentious, pointless or silly – usually because they have read very little and perhaps were put off by misguided or bad teaching at school!

Yet, many young people – both boys and girls – say that they do like poetry, so the trick is to harness that enjoyment and relate it to general reading as part of the totality of wide-ranging literacy skills.

The aim, remember, is to nurture the ability to read absolutely anything the pupils are given or want to read – effortlessly, appreciatively and with an appropriate level of comprehension.

That means giving poetry reading plenty of status in school. One way for teachers to do that is to structure lots of activities around poetry – in primary classrooms and in secondary English lessons, of course, but there is scope for weaving poetry into other parts of the curriculum too. What's to stop a geography specialist having a poster of Roy Campbell's 'Zebras' on his/her classroom wall? A science teacher, too, might find 'The Dissection' by Colin Rowbotham a useful focus for discussion.

There is plenty of poetry relevant to history, RE, PSHE, art, music, and almost every other subject too. There are, for example, poetry collections dedicated to football by John Foster, Paul Cookson and Tony Bradman, among others.

Try these ten things to do with a poem:

1 Turn it into an improvised (or rehearsed) play.
2 Use it as a starting point for pupils' own writing (poetry or prose).
3 Share it with the rest of the school in an assembly.
4 Encourage children to read it aloud in pairs, using different voices and accents.
5 Let children devise a set of questions about it and give them to another pupil to answer.
6 Search for other poems like it, for example on the same subject or by the same poet.
7 Learn it by heart.
8 Set it to music.
9 Paint, draw or sculpt something inspired by it.
10 Write it out, illustrate or decorate it and give it to someone as a gift.

Application

Letting poetry trigger other reading

Many young people enjoy creating their own poetry anthologies. Anyone who finds a poem s/he really likes can feel the urge to 'capture' it in some way and keep it for reading again later.

Traditionally, creating a personal anthology meant copying the poem out in a special notebook or on a sheet to put in a folder. And that, of course, is still fine if it appeals.

Making electronic copies is another possibility. Poems can be typed out and then printed in a creatively wide range of fonts (and colours) for inclusion in a ring binder, or stored in a computer folder.

However it is done, the development of an anthology builds quite a reading resource for the creator – and sometimes he or she can share it with others so that the anthology helps to build enthusiasm for reading, and reading skills, of others in the group or class.

Teachers should make a poetry collection too. Then they can share their anthology with the pupils and role-model a real love of poetry reading which some pupils will then want to emulate.

For secondary students in particular, another reading possibility which comes from an interest in poetry is wanting to know – and then researching and reading about – the lives of the poets behind the poetry – some of whom have lived extraordinary, colourful lives.

A word about copyright. If a poet has been dead for 70 years or more the copyright on his or her work has expired. If the work is more recent, there is no law against making a copy for your own use, but it must not be otherwise stored, sold or published without permission.

Advice

There is plenty of information about poets' lives in biographies, companions to English literature, encyclopedias and on the internet. The following is just a tiny selection of poets whose life stories might interest students.

- Elizabeth Barrett Browning, who eloped aged 40 with the poet Robert Browning (and bore a child), having always been an invalid.

- Percy Bysshe Shelley, who was expelled from university, then, already married, eloped with a girl of 17 (who later drowned herself), then married Mary (author of *Frankenstein*) and drowned at age 30.

- Ted Hughes, whose wife Sylvia Plath, another poet, committed suicide.

- John Clare, who had serious mental health problems.

- John Keats, who died of a lung disease aged only 26.

- Christina Rossetti, who wrote passionate religious poetry and was the sister of famous painter Dante Gabriel Rossetti.

- Walter Raleigh, who was executed on the orders of the king.

- Samuel Taylor Coleridge, who was a debt-ridden drug addict.

- Maya Angelou, who as a child didn't speak for five years, became a cable-car conductor and gave birth to a son at age 16, before becoming a civil rights campaigner and university professor.

Reading about poets as well as reading their poetry is another way of becoming a more fluent reader.

Group play-reading

Exploring a play in a group is a good way of getting everyone reading.

The ideal way of doing this is to choose and browse through the play – or a section of it – in advance. If parts are allocated early, pupils can take scripts home and do a bit of preparation. This means more independent reading, and will almost certainly lead to a better play-reading in class.

It is quite easy to involve everyone in the group by choosing a play with a lot of parts or by sharing them out. If you are reading Harold Brighouse's *Hobson's Choice* (Heinemann), for instance, Student A can be Maggie in Act 1, Student B can play her in Act 2, and so on.

If you have children who are really reluctant to read a part, it is best not to force it. Just make sure that there are enough copies of the script for everyone to have one. Then all students are reading because they are all following even if they are not reading aloud. In modern plays, there are often quite extensive stage directions, and these too have to be read silently by everyone present in order for the play to make sense.

Play-reading doesn't have to be exclusive to English or drama lessons. It can be part of cross-curricular work in primary classes. And there are plenty of plays which have something to say in other specialist lessons in secondary school. *The Gift* by Nicola Baldwin, for example, is about genetics and could be used in science (download the script from geneticfutures.com/thegift/play/author.asp). Robert Bolt's *A Man for All Seasons* (A&C Black/Methuen Drama) is a must for history classes working on the Tudors. Any play written or adapted by David Wood has potential for primary school reading.

Advice

These are just a few suggestions for plays suitable for group reading:

Under 12

- *The Gingerbread Man* by David Wood (Samuel French)
- *Alice in Wonderland* (various adaptations)
- *You Made Me* by Kelvin Reynolds and Adrian Lockwood (Collins)
- *Babe, the Sheep-Pig* adapted from Dick King-Smith by David Wood (Samuel French)
- *Charlie and the Chocolate Factory* adapted from Roald Dahl by Richard R. George (Puffin)

12+

- *Two Plays for Young People* (*Fairytaleheart and Sparkleshark*) by Philip Ridley (Faber and Faber)
- *Under Milk Wood* by Dylan Thomas (Penguin)
- *Blithe Spirit* by Noël Coward (various publishers)
- *The History Boys* by Alan Bennett (Faber and Faber)
- *Amadeus* by Peter Shaffer (HarperPerennial)

Application

Poets and playwrights in school

Many schools invite fiction writers into school to take part in book weeks, days or festivals or to contribute to curriculum enrichment. It makes sense to invite poets and playwrights too.

Many poets see school visits as part of their work, and it is sometimes possible to get external funding to help pay for it. If not, try local sponsors or the parents' association, or try to persuade the school bursar or business manager to factor some author visits (all genres) into the school's budget.

Poets who engage well with young people include Grace Nicholls, Wendy Cope and Kit Wright.

Playwrights who specialize in writing or adapting plays likely to appeal to under-14s include Charles Way, Vicky Ireland, Mike Kenny and Abi Brown.

Like novelists, poets and playwrights can be contacted via their publishers. Some have individual websites with contact details.

Once a poet or playwright has agreed to visit your school, discuss his or her preferences for the way the visit is organized. Students in rows or in the round? Should the children prepare anything? Is the speaker willing to answer questions? Bear in mind that the details of these arrangements will depend partly on the age of the children.

Tell your local newspaper that the poet/playwright is coming. Such events tend to make good copy and it is positive publicity for the school. If you are interviewed for the paper, you can stress the importance of wider reading and building up reading skills.

 The secret to a successful visit lies in meticulous preparation!

To prepare for a poet's visit:

- Read with the children as many of the poet's poems as possible, and encourage them to read his/her poems independently.

- Encourage children to read as widely as possible about the poet's life, background and achievements. The internet is probably the best source, particularly if the poet has his/her own website.

- Ask the poet or his/her publisher for a CV or brief biography in advance, and make sure that pupils have read it before the visit.

- Sell some of the poet's books in school beforehand (you can probably get them from the publisher or a bookshop on sale or return). With books in hand, the children are even more likely to read the poems.

- Then, when the poet comes, he or she can be asked to sign the children's copies. (Most are more than happy to do this.)

- Make arrangements for children to be able to buy poetry books which the poet will almost certainly bring with him/her for sale.

- Invite parents, other staff, pupils from other schools, local librarians and so on to the session. It helps to keep the cost down if you spread it around, and the greater involvement raises the status and profile of the visit.

To prepare for a playwright's visit:

- Make sure the children know as much of the writer's work as possible.

- Organize group play-readings.

- Take the children to the theatre to see a work by the playwright being performed.

- Show a DVD adaptation of one of the writer's plays.

- Encourage the children to buy texts of the plays so that they can ask the playwright to sign them.

- Talk to the children about the sorts of question they want to/can/should ask the playwright.

Theatre trips and reading

Much great theatre for young audiences is rooted in novels. So, if you can get your learners to the theatre, there is a double bonus in the encouragement of reading.

First, if they know they are going to see a play based on a book there is a big incentive – which you can reinforce – to read the book beforehand.

Second, if they see a play and enjoy it but have not yet read the book it is based on, many will want to hang on to the theatre experience by reading the book afterwards.

That is why the National Theatre in London, for example, sells the novels that its children's plays are based on in its bookshop and sometimes on stands just outside the auditorium.

A reader who is intrigued by the conversion of novels into plays (and it is a very interesting subject) can look at the playscript as well as the novel.

Big organizations like the National Theatre also tend to have a good education website (see Stagework at nationaltheatre.org.uk) where students can read even more background information.

Theatre programmes or playbills – although often a bit pricey in the UK, they are usually free in the USA – are another useful source of relevant reading matter.

Nearly all theatre companies mount an occasional children's play – typically at Christmas. But there are theatres (Polka and Unicorn in London; All Children's Theatre, Rhode Island and Oklahoma Children's Theatre in the USA) and touring groups (such as Quicksilver and Kazzum in the UK) which specialize in work for children and young people.

Don't forget that older students can watch carefully chosen mainstream theatre.

Advice

The following list suggests some of the many recent plays based on books which have the potential to get young people reading more and thereby developing their literacy skills.

- *Coram Boy* adapted by Helen Edmundson from Jamila Gavin's novel (Heinemann)
- *His Dark Materials* adapted by Nicholas Wright from Philip Pullman's trilogy (Nick Hern Books)
- *Journey to the River Sea* adapted by Carl Miller from Eva Ibbotson's novel
- *The Witches* adapted by David Wood from Roald Dahl's novel (Puffin)
- *Oz* adapted by Patrick Shanahan from Frank L. Baum's novel and his notes on the way he might have created a theatre version
- *The Sword in the Stone* adapted by Rachel King from T.H. White's novel
- *The Wind in the Willows* adapted by Alan Bennett from Kenneth Graeme's novel (Faber and Faber)

New novel- or story-based plays are appearing all the time in theatres, especially at Christmas. *A Christmas Carol*, *Great Expectations*, *Pride and Prejudice*, *Jane Eyre* and similar classics have been dramatized for the stage many times. Sometimes, particularly if the production company is a small one, the adaptation might be written by, say, the director and will not be published. Nonetheless, there is still an incentive for the audience to read for the first time, or to return to, the book which inspired the play.

You could read the novel with a group before taking them to see the play. Or begin reading the novel together to get children interested and then set them off to finish the book independently, before or after seeing a performance.

Visiting theatre groups

Taking children to the theatre is expensive even with group discounts because travel has to be costed in. Arrangements can be difficult or impossible in far-flung rural areas or where families cannot afford to contribute.

A much cheaper option, which can have the same reading-related benefits, is to bring a theatre group into school.

There are no travel costs, and there is the bonus of no time-consuming administrative work such as completing risk-assessment forms for pupils going off site.

Typically, a visiting theatre company charges a flat rate – say £500 or $1,000. If a large number of pupils watch the performance, the cost per head is relatively low (and you can always share it with another school) and may be manageable within the school budget, unlike off-site theatre visits which are usually treated as extra-curricular activities that need parental contributions to make them viable.

If you find a company offering a book-related performance there are all the same advantages of motivating the pupils to read the book before and/or afterwards.

Another advantage of having the theatre come to you is that it is very immediate. Pupils often get the chance to meet the actors or take part in a workshop in a way which would be unlikely at a regular theatre performance.

Exeter University drama department's website has a useful list of UK theatre companies which visit schools: spa.ex.ac.uk/drama/links/theatreedu.html

The Rogues and Vagabonds theatre-lovers' site (roguesandvagabonds.co.uk/Theatre/childrens_theatres.html) lists children's theatre groups and other useful contacts.

Invite a theatre group offering a mobile production of *The Silver Sword*, based on the novel by Ian Serraillier and suitable for almost all children from about age nine. It is a Second World War story set in Europe, and adults like it too. Treat it as a project.

Before the big day, do everything you can to make sure every child has read the book. You could:

- read sections aloud to get their interest
- make copies available in the classroom for borrowing
- have copies on sale
- ask children who have already read it to talk to others – give oral reviews.

Try to encourage spin-off reading by getting pupils to read more widely about displaced children, refugees (in various countries) and about the Second World War in general.

Relevant fiction includes:

- *Little Soldier* by Bernard Ashley (Orchard; also available from Heinemann as a playscript)
- *Postcards From No Man's Land* by Aidan Chambers (Red Fox)
- *Give Me Shelter* edited by Tony Bradman (Frances Lincoln)
- *Goodnight Mister Tom* by Michelle Magorian (Puffin)
- *I am David* by Ann Holm (Mammoth)
- *The Other Side of Truth* by Beverley Naidoo (Puffin)
- *Girl in Red* by Gaye Hicyilmaz (Orion)
- *The Breadwinner* by Deborah Ellis (OUP)
- *Oranges in No Man's Land* by Elizabeth Laird (Macmillan).

Learners could also, with your guidance and encouragement, read about these topics in newspapers, magazines and on the internet.

After seeing the play, they could find out more about Ian Seraillier and his work.

By then, anyone who didn't quite get engaged with reading *The Silver Sword* might now feel inspired to do so.

Application

77

5

Reading motivators

Reading incentive schemes

Some schools are experimenting with points or reward schemes (a bit like supermarket loyalty cards) to persuade children to read more books and to build up their reading stamina.

The idea is that the more books a child reads the more points (or similar) s/he gets. These then lead to some sort of reward, such as prizes, certificates or credit at the school bookshop. One difficulty with such a scheme, however, is finding a way of checking that the books really have been read.

Accelerated Reader, part of Renaissance Learning, is one way of making monitoring easier for schools, and it provides a good example of such an idea in action. It is an American scheme operating in 70,000 schools worldwide. See renaissance-learning.co.uk.

Basically, Accelerated Reader is a computer program which includes carefully thought-out quizzes on thousands of books – from the simplest picture book through to long novels by Charles Dickens and Jane Austen.

First, the reader takes a computerized test to find out what level he or she should be reading at and then borrows and reads a book listed with the appropriate colour coding. Once the book is read, the pupil completes a very searching computer quiz which checks that the book really has been read and understood. Only then can the pupil move on to another book.

Children seem to enjoy doing this and in most participating schools they receive rewards for reading more than a certain number of books or for progressing up a level.

Advice

Make the most of any scheme you find – or can invent – which provides an incentive for children to read. From sponsored reading to best-book votes, it all raises the status and appeal of reading in pupils' minds.

You know your learners. What sort of reward would motivate them to read more books? And what can school funds run to?

All of the following rewards have worked for some pupils in some schools:

- Slices of pizza or other edibles (but aim to offer healthy snacks).
- A group sleep-in at school on a weekend.
- A paid-for (so no cost to the children's families) theatre trip.
- Credit for local shops (ideal if you can persuade a retail outlet to sponsor the scheme).
- Stickers and stars (for the youngest children).
- Lots of public praise.
- Name(s) published (in school magazines on the intranet, on the main noticeboard in the reception area/lobby, read out in assembly and so on).

School Libraries Online at iasl-slo/org/readprom.html suggests internet resources for promoting reading in the USA. There are plenty of good tried-and-tested, yet adaptable, ideas here.

Application

Holding a sponsored read

Young people are often motivated to read more if they know that their reading is not only an enjoyable way of developing themselves, but also helping to make a real difference to people in need. One way of harnessing this enthusiasm is to hold a sponsored read. It is a tool that works for any age group.

Consider Readathon (readathon.org) as the basis of your sponsored read. It is a charity which provides support for sponsored reading events and raises funds for children's cancer charity CLIC Sargent (clicsargent.org.uk) and the Roald Dahl Foundation (roalddahlfoundation.org).

Readathon, of which Roald Dahl was chairman from 1988 until his death in 1990, was started in 1984 to encourage reading. The money it raises helps children with cancer, Hodgkin's disease, leukaemia, epilepsy, blood disorders and acquired brain injury.

Although it is ideal for Children's Book Week in October, you can hold a readathon at any time of the year.

The organization supplies a free pack containing:

- sponsorship forms
- badges, stickers and other extras for participants
- literacy-based project materials
- coloured posters
- organizer's guide.

Another scheme is the Read Across America programme run by the National Education Association (nea.org/readacross). It encourages schools, children and parents to get more involved in book-related activities including sponsored reads. Like Readathon, it supplies resources to help with running events and activities.

Advice

To organize a sponsored read you need to:

- Work with a single class or group, or get the support of colleagues to make it a school-wide activity.

- Identify a charity you and the children want to support.

- Decide whether you will allow children to read any book(s) they choose or whether to have a set list – perhaps of titles the school has multiple copies of.

- Fix on a time span – one week, two weeks, a month?

- Think of a way of certifying that each book has been read – perhaps a parent or teacher could sign a confirmation. Or you could set aside time in school, say every day for a month, so that you can establish that reading has been done. If you are really brave, have plenty of adults to help you, and can do without sleep, you could consider a 24-hour sponsored 'read-in' at a weekend!

- Devise or source the paperwork – sponsorship forms and check lists to record the reading log on.

- Encourage the children to get as many sponsors as possible. The simplest way is to be sponsored so much per book. Sometimes the time spent reading can be sponsored at, perhaps,1p per minute, but this is fiddly to monitor unless you say nothing less than 20 minutes counts. However, it can allow slower readers to take part on an equal basis.

- Have a reasonably foolproof way of collecting the proceeds afterwards.

- Take part yourself – with sponsors – so that it becomes 'our' project.

Following book prizes

There are several awards for children's books which are awarded annually – Nestlé Prize (formerly Smarties Prize) and Costa Book of the Year (formerly the Whitbread Prize), for example, and in the USA, the Newbery Medal.

Drawing young readers' attention to these, and encouraging them to read and discuss the shortlisted books before the winner is announced, is another way of keeping them interested in books.

In the UK, the Carnegie Medal, for instance, has been awarded annually for a children's book since 1936. Past winners include *Pigeon Post* by Arthur Ransome, *The Borrowers* by Mary Norton, *The Owl Service* by Alan Garner and *Storm* by Kevin Crossley-Holland. Anne Fine, Jan Mark and Peter Dickinson have all won it twice. It is now run in conjunction with the Kate Greenaway Medal by the Chartered Institute of Librarians and Information Professionals (CILIP).

The large judging panel consists of children's librarians. They announce their shortlist of five to eight books each April – chosen from books published between January and August the previous year.

In recent years, many schools have signed up to be Carnegie Medal 'shadowers'. This means that the school children read the books, discuss them in their schools and post reviews on CILIP's website. CILIP provides advice and support materials for those wanting to take part.

When the medal winner is announced in June, readers who have shadowed the prize take a real interest because they feel involved and have chosen their own winner. This is something like the bookish equivalent of watching the fortunes of the football team they support.

The only resource needed is copies of the shortlisted books. For details of the shadowing scheme, visit carnegiegreenaway.org.uk/shadowingsite

Advice

If you want to follow a book prize other than the Carnegie Medal:

- Check relevant websites to find out exactly when a shortlist is announced.

- Make sure you know which books are on the list as soon as it is published.

- Assess the budget in advance for funds to buy copies of the books. (Can you persuade a local bookseller to sponsor this?)

- Ideally, you need about 50 per cent more books than you have pupils because they will read at different speeds and you don't want anyone left bookless.

- Read all the books yourself.

- Know when the overall winner will be announced (check websites). That is your deadline. Build the pupils up to it and make the most of the sense of anticipation.

- Ask pupils to record their responses, perhaps by writing reviews, putting comments on a class or library noticeboard, giving them a pro forma, setting up an area of the intranet – whatever works for you.

- If possible, arrange 'book group' times for readers to discuss their thoughts.

- Organize a pupil vote for the winner on the day before the award announcement is due.

- Then, on the big day, compare your votes with the actual winner – and discuss, dispute, celebrate, marvel...

World Book Day

World Book Day, which began in 1997, is usually on the first Thursday in March, but you will need to check the date from year to year. Sponsored in the UK and Ireland by National Book Tokens and the Booksellers' Association, it is a celebration of the importance and pleasure of books, accompanied by lots of events. See worldbookday.com

Schools can register to receive packs and free book tokens worth £1 for pupils. Each year, a small number of 'bargain' books are published – usually by well-known authors. They cost just £1 so there are at least some books for children to spend their tokens on if they don't want to or can't add any more money to the value of the token.

In 2005, World Book Day – which is a charity – extended its remit to involve very young children. By 2006, 11,000 pre-school organizations, such as nursery schools, had registered. Numbers still grow each year.

On the day, World Book Day publishes a list of quick reads to encourage and inspire 'those of us who have lost the habit of reading for pleasure or have yet to acquire it'. Many of your pupils will be in the latter category, so World Book Day is a very useful thing to get involved in.

Advice

Lead an assembly for World Book Day.

Show the audience a) the Authorised Version of the Bible (1611) and b) the Qur'an – probably the two most important books ever written because they have influenced, in very significant ways, so many people over such a long time. Say a bit about each of them.

The world's most influential secular book is probably the *Complete Works of Shakespeare*. Show a copy and say a bit about it.

Then show a copy of your own favourite book, ideally suitable for the age group of your learners. It doesn't matter if it is a rarity or a classic such as *The Wind in the Willows*, *Gone With the Wind*, *Rebecca*, *The Silver Sword*, *Watership Down*, *Winnie-the-Pooh*... as long as you can explain why you love it.

Talk about your book for a few minutes and recommend it.

Have ten students primed to stand up one by one and say the title and author of a book they would like to recommend on World Book Day – in the form of an oral list.

So, you will need:

- the Bible
- the Qur'an
- an edition of the complete Shakespeare
- your favourite book
- students' titles organized.

Make sure that:

- the list of the students' book choices, together with the one you recommend, are displayed afterwards all over the school
- the school library has plenty of copies of these books – set this up in advance.

Library clubs

It is now common practice for schools – at both primary and secondary level – to enrich the curriculum through after-school clubs.

In any school which is serious about promoting wider reading (and there shouldn't be a school anywhere which isn't) one of these should be a library club.

The simple idea of a library club is to get children into the library (or library area or book corner) for an hour or so after school to read and take part in book-related activities. For example, as well as 'just' reading, they might listen to audiobooks, do quizzes about books, design illustrations for books, write letters to authors, learn how to find what they want in the library, research book reviews and author biographies on the internet, listen to talks by authors or tell each other about books which have impressed them and they would like to recommend.

In a secondary school, the club might be the province of the school librarian or the teacher who runs the library. In a smaller primary school, it is likely to be any teacher with the enthusiasm. Either way, you need a 'book nut' at the helm. Remember that the club may be competing for children's time and enthusiasm with a football, drama or art club – all of which are potentially more attractive to young eyes.

Some readers are very happy to curl up in a corner with a book they are already engaged with. That's fine. Let them. Others may want to talk about books and/or take part in something more active. The key thing is to keep children interested in books and to keep them coming to the club. If you are really successful, the children will enjoy themselves so much that they will tell their friends what a good time they have at library club and your numbers will rise.

Advice

Get as many other adults as you can to come along to your library club – it reinforces the message that adult reading is not exclusive to librarians and English teachers. Invite classroom assistants, domestic staff and colleagues who teach subjects like science and PE. Role-modelling, as we've noted before, is a very effective way of promoting the behaviour you want – in this case reading and otherwise engaging with books and literature.

 Organize an activity or clear focus for each club meeting. You might:

- set up a literary treasure hunt (different characters and locations in various books on the shelves)
- read the opening of a really gripping book aloud, such as Bernard Ashley's *Little Soldier* (Orchard), Deborah Ellis's *The Breadwinner* (OUP) or Beverley Naidoo's *Web of Lies* (Puffin), and stop on a cliffhanger
- watch a short section of a DVD version of a book together
- ask a 'non-literary' colleague (such as the head of ICT) to talk about his or her favourite book.

Provide some refreshments. A couple of packets of biscuits with something as simple as juice in a paper cup will do. Find a way of budgeting for this – it really helps to make your club feel more 'clubby' and less like a lesson.

Always have something exciting planned for next week and tell the children about it to encourage them to keep coming.

Advertise the club and the next meeting's activity on posters around school, in the weekly newsletter and/or on the intranet.

Consider asking parents to come to the club too. If you get them onside and show them what you are doing they are more likely to encourage their children to continue their membership and to read at home.

Application

Book groups

Book groups have become quite popular with adults in the UK, the USA and elsewhere. Indeed, the plot of Karen Joy Fowler's 2005 novel *The Jane Austen Book Club* depends on one!

In a book group – of friends, work colleagues or however it is formed – everyone reads an agreed book and then they hold an informal meeting to have a structured discussion about their reading.

Typically, members take turns to suggest book titles to the group and/or members might vote on which book they want to read for the next discussion session. Usually, someone agrees to lead, or chair, the discussion.

A similar system can work very well in schools at all levels – and is a good way of steering children into wider reading beyond the narrow limits of what they have to study for tests and coursework.

Ideally, the students, especially at 12 and older, should be able to manage the group themselves with minimum guidance and supervision, although input from a teacher can often revive a flagging discussion.

Once a book group is established, it makes sense to 'publish' (in school newsletters, on the intranet and so on) some of its views about the books it has covered. Its activities can then help to promote reading – even in pupils who don't belong to the book group.

About ten is probably the maximum size for a workable book group. Any larger, and some people will be marginalised in discussion. If there are lots of keen participants, set up more than one group.

Children will (and should) come up with good titles of their own, but bear in mind, and point out, that a selected book needs to be 'meaty' enough to generate talking points. Here are a few suggestions of books which offer plenty of scope for discussion (age indications are only an approximate guide):

8+

Simone's Diary by Helena Pielichaty (OUP)
The Cat Mummy by Jacqueline Wilson (Corgi)

10+

The Tulip Touch by Anne Fine (Puffin)
Holes by Louis Sachar (Bloomsbury)

11+

A Gathering Light by Jennifer Donnelly (Bloomsbury)
The Garbage King by Elizabeth Laird (Macmillan)

12+

Angel Blood by John Singleton (Ladybird)

14+

Junk by Melvyn Burgess (Puffin)

16+

My Sister's Keeper by Jodi Picoult (Hodder and Stoughton)

Possible talking points include:
- plot, how it works and how the author has presented it
- characters, how they are shown and whether they are convincing
- the writer's style
- moral points and other issues raised by the story
- How it compares with other books.

Application

Further reading and other sources of information

The Oxford Companion to Children's Literature
Carpenter and Mari Pritchard is a good source of information about children's books from various periods and countries.

Rainbow Readers from Ransom is a series of 26 books with 54 accompanying activities for children who are struggling to learn to read (http://actinic.thwd.co.uk).

Boys Rule and Girls Rock is a series for SEN children published by Rising Stars (risingstars-uk.com).

Lovereading (lovereading.co.uk) has a lot of up to date information about books, recommendations and downloadable extracts. See also the sister sites lovereading4kids and lovereading4schools.

Useful books suggesting further tools and techniques are *Really Want to Learn English* (Books 1, 2 and 3) by Susan Elkin (Galore Park) and *Getting the Buggers to Read*